Journey

Poems of Love, Laughter and Nature Along Life's Pathways

Joan LaRose

Journey: Poems of Love, Laughter and
Nature Along Life's Pathways
by Joan A. LaRose

First Edition - 2014

ISBN-13: 978-1497315679
ISBN-10: 1497315670

Printed in the United States of America

Hitchcock Lake Publications
edited by Chuck Miceli and Michael Lyman

This book is dedicated to my children, grandchildren and great-grandchildren.

It is a tribute which entwines my past with their future.

Acknowledgements

This collection of poems reflects a gathering of wisdom and experience from people I have had the privilege of journeying through life with. These pages are filled with their stories and mine. I wish to thank the poetry corner at Southington Care Center for their encouragement and support, especially: Julie Norko, Marion Gifford, Lillian Olsen, Phyllis Knipe and Stacy Carleton.

Particular thanks to Chuck Miceli, mentor, motivator and editor. Also special thanks to Michael Lyman, co-editor and proofreader. Their gifts of time and talent made this book possible.

Introduction

I have heard it said that tears of sorrow and pain are composed of different chemicals than are those of laughter and joy. I have no scientific knowledge of this, yet I believe it to be true. Laughter, joy, pain, and sorrow have given birth to the poetry in this book. When hurt has no place to dissipate itself, when laughter begs to be shared and multiplied with others, pen and paper are healing tools that I find invaluable to express, release, and share life's emotions. In some ways we are all conduits for enriching relationships. When pain flows like a river or laughter babbles like a brook, words and sounds give forth life. That, to me, is poetry.

Joan LaRose

Table of Contents

Life

Laughter

Love

Nature

Journey

Precious Boy

(For my great-grandson Isaac)

Precious boy, dancing in sweet
embryonic nectar. Miracle
and mystery to all who await you.
New life growing stronger each day.

We welcome you, hope for the
future, safe in the embrace
of Mama's womb. Your journey
has begun soon to lead you
to our nurturing arms.

Until then, little one, we wait
in joyful anticipation.

The Great Depression

With tear stained cheeks, hunger gnawing

at her belly, back and forth she sways

in the old rocking chair as if traveling

away from desperation. She holds her child

tightly, trying to protect him from reality.

In faltering voice she sings to him. A nursery

rhyme:

Old Mother Hubbard...Went to the cupboard...

The boy looks up at cracked ceilings darkened

by a coal stove...*To get her poor dog a bone.*

Back and forth she rocks as if calming his hunger

...And so the poor dog had none.

Daddy walks through the door of the small

tenement with shame in his eyes, clings,

to a loaf of bread. "I stole it," he said

in a voice barely audible. The boy will

eat today, tomorrow...perhaps. The day after?

Tenements

Weathered tenements scented
with savory, ethnic fare,
as cauldrons into which are poured
Old World spice with care.

Aromas wafting through each door
symbolic in their blending,
of customs shared so proudly,
of friendship never ending.

My mother's Polish-baked delights,
the Kelly's Irish stew,
the tantalizing French cuisine,
a culinary few.

The tangy peppers hung to dry
for slowly simmering sauce,
once calmed our hunger—now the soul
with reminiscent thoughts.

Each evening meal a festival
with stories shared by all,
'round tables filled with laughter
heard throughout the shabby halls.

With porches runged and banistered
from where on glory day,
as sparks migrated toward the skies
I witnessed New-World ways.

Where melodies of broken verse
in symphony resound,
and anthems linger reverently
my heritage abounds.

Tradition paled through time and place
so graciously departs
the precious gift my parents gave
remaining in my heart.

Skating with Carolyn

Adjusting my skate with metal key,

I discover winter's growth in me.

Not too loose and not too tight,

My roller skates must fit just right.

Melted snow, warm spring day.

Metal skates ready for play.

Well-oiled wheels roll round the block:

Ward Street, Lawrence, Broad and Park.

We glide along the smooth concrete,

An urban rink beneath our feet.

Long hair flailing, feeling free,

We're speeding by for all to see.

Sister Reginette

Here's to Sister Reginette,
a pious holy soul.
She taught us well, self-discipline,
our spirits to control.

We knelt at Mass not questioning
the holy will of God,
obeying because Sister said,
with passive, fearful nod.

Emotional virginity,
no anger, joy or pain.
We held ourselves as hostages
"good" boys and girls remained.

Here's to Tommy, Pat and me!
How did we make it through?
It must have been the grace of God,
perhaps for Sister—too?

Ritual

It always begins this way. Eerie wails
of mournful sirens raid my solace.
My father sprints from a chair, removes
shades from the closet, quickly covers
windows as each light is eclipsed.
My older brother finds this exciting.
Knots of fear lodge in my stomach.
"Where is Mommy?"

It's strange how darkness turns
voices to a whisper. There is talk
of nylon stockings, rationed
meat, victory gardens, fireside
chats and war bonds. I wonder
what an "FDR" is? The sirens
wail again. Relief at last!

No planes—not this time.

All is well once more. Through

transparent windows streetlights

glow. Conversation and laughter

revisit. We turn the radio on

and listen to Superman while

my mother makes popcorn

as if nothing happened.

Great-Grandchild

(For my great-granddaughter Colletta)

Today I looked into my future

One that is bright with

Anticipation and promise

Its color is as blue as the eyes

Of a newborn baby girl,

Pink as her rose-tinted cheeks, gold as the
locks of her hair.

It will blossom as she grows

And bloom as she sprinkles laughter,

And love to all she touches.

Such joy to share the essence of life once
lived

And then once more through the child of my
child.

My gift to the future,

Becoming one and the same for me.

Obsession

Thoughts like errant children locked
in the cells of my brain, undisciplined.
I endure the tantrums, prisoners
demanding endless attention.

Some command me to act on compulsion.
Others, like rats scurry through a gray
maze in search of release. They all carry
on, ignoring a simple word: **STOP**.

Words

I love to play with words
> like monotonous and melodious
> that describe what they mean by simply
> saying them.

Those that have multiple meanings:
> "run" and "short", "slip" and "court".

Obscene words which give dramatic power
> until overused.

Sacred morsels which try to describe the
indescribable
> but never quite succeed.

Snippets of prose that rhyme
> like "sneeze" and "freeze", "lost" and
> "frost", "cream" and "dream".

My favorites are Dr. Seuss words:

    "pantookas" and "frazzles", "gizmos" and

    "drazzles".

Colloquialisms

    such as "doohickey", "blah, blah, blah",

    "yadda, yadda, yadda,

    and the olde "huzzah".

Words with a foreign ambiance

    like—well ambiance.

    Those borrowed bits of ethnicity:

    "sayonara", "expresso", "coup d'état", and

    "pro bono".

And so, in a word, FIN.

Charlotte's Garden

Charlotte has a garden where her prized possessions
bloom,
Within her heart they blossom in a very special room.

A room of deep contentment with flowers none the
same.
Each has a special corner and a very special name.

There's Connor and Colleen, her Irish lad and lassie.
Christina, ladylike and sweet, and Kyla pert and sassy.

You'll see in Charlotte's garden a lovely, winding Rose
Who wraps her love 'round grandma's heart as
beautifully she grows.

A teddy bear is Joshua with hair so red and curly,
Her "teddy bear" he'll always be though he grow big
and burly.

Now David was the first to bloom a rustic oak is he,
With branches spread beyond the wall a strong and
sturdy tree.

Melissa, now a woman, such a sweet and fragrant
blossom,
And Gregory, her younger sib with acting talents
awesome.

In Charlotte's garden sprouts a bloom with double
treats and tricks.
A two-fold package from the stork are Benjamin and
Nick!

There's Mikey who's a fine young man, feet rooted in
the ground.
Along the garden path he walks where joy and love
abound.

Ah who's this fine equestrian amidst this floral vision?
It's none but Taylor strutting by with confident
precision.

A name so lovely next is Erin, shamrocks all around
her,
Twas in the verdant, fragrant grass that Charlotte one
day found her.

A King intrepid Adam is, no shrinking violet he,
Yet 'neath the petals he displays a sensitivity.

When Charlotte's world seems filled with gloom, she
walks through garden gate
To calm her loneliness and fear and all her cares abate.

How fortunate is she to have this lovely get-a-way
Where all her cares turn into blooms each cold and
wintry day.

Gift

Giving holds pleasure.
The giver offers a gift
anticipating.

The gift becomes real
with true generosity
blessing the giver.

Gracious acceptance
completes the ceremony's
sacred ritual.

Time is Up

Fix it, fix it, clean it, shine it,

stir it, mix it, pay it, sign it.

Earn it, buy it, then prepare it.

If it breaks I must repair it.

Plan it, do it, must succeed.

Make it happen, do the deed.

Heed the ad, go out and buy it.

Mend it, sew it, wash and dry it.

Have it, own it, keep it, train it.

It's all yours, you must maintain it.

Plant it, hoe it, water 'n' weed it.

Grow it, pick it, blend and knead it.

Time is up, it went so fast.

I never danced, or sang or laughed.

Laughter

Soliloquy

I've yet to write a poem with words

Like "thee" and "thou" and "yonder"

Shakespearean soliloquys on which

The readers ponder

A "dost" or "doth" have not a place

In my vocabulary

Although I'm sure they can be

Found in Webster's dictionary

When asked why I avoid such

Words as "'tis", "anon"

And "bleaketh"

I say I need to understand the

Verse of which I speaketh

 Poet

I thought a moment, then a while.
Soon moments turned to hours.
Just contemplating poetry
to write about the flowers.

The rose is quite pretentious
and violets very shy.
The sunflower soars upward
as it reaches for the sky.

Snapdragons too cantankerous,
Sweet William much too sweet.
The lowly dandelion a weed
That grows beneath my feet.

I thought again and realized
when all is said and done,
of all the poets in the world
I'm certainly not one!

Yellow Pad

Today I bought a brand new
yellow pad, legal-size and lined.
One can't write creatively on plain
white paper. It lacks the character
And structure of the impressive legal pad.

The words seem to take on so much
more meaning. Adjectives more descriptive,
verbs jump off the page, penmanship
almost legible. The authoritative double
red line at the left margin has no mercy
for writers' block. Somewhere is a poem
begging to be written waiting
for the proper venue, the yellow pad.

Ode To An Elastic Band

Oh simple elastic band
so rarely recognized for your
service in the name of efficiency,
your achievements are countless.

Your smooth surface girdles
dozens of pencils together.
You have prevented many
a childhood pigtail from
coming undone.

Right up there with staplers
and paper clips, fearlessly
you stretch your limits.
Occasionally breaking in
the line of duty. I applaud you.

Brain Lock

In some remote corner? Under the bed?
Inside the closet, I hope she's not dead!
Find her I must, this great ball of fur!

Is she out in the hall, stuck in a drawer,
napping somewhere outside the door?
Find her I must, my mischievous pet!

Perhaps in the basement or out on the lawn,
or up in a tree. Where has she gone?
Find her I must, this adventurous cat!

She's hiding discretely on leonine perch,
observing somewhere as I frantically search.
Find her I must, my camouflaged culprit!

She hears me I'm sure meowing her name.
Is she not feeling well or playing a game?
Find her I must, oh troublesome creature!

My brain locks in thought of this feline's location.
She's ignoring my calls of frantic persuasion.
Find her I must, this silly old cat!

At the end of the day she calmly appears.
My obsession moves on to some other fear.
Did I lose my glasses somewhere–maybe here?

Pot Luck

Gone are the days of impressing the crowd
A few dozen brownies will do.
No need to prepare fancy, frivolous fare
Of recipes daring and new.

I once would deliberate hours on end
When asked for a simple confection.
I'd buy the ingredients, bake up a storm
Dreaming visions of sugared perfection.

No more will these hands give the 200 strokes
Which Ms. Crocker requires precisely.
I'll go to the bakery where strudel awaits
And satisfy palates quite nicely.

Next Life

Next Life,

   I would like to be an otter.

   Carefree, spontaneous antics,

   splashing, fur soaked, no thought

   of yesterday or tomorrow.

   I would dive, swim

   this way and that, back

   flip with other happy otters.

   No disrespect for the busy beaver

   or bee, I so wish to be foolish

   and fancy free, glide through

   life–far too important to take

   seriously. Would you

   like to come be an otter with me?

Love

Fragrant Gardenias

I took several deep breaths and dialed,
almost hung up, then heard your voice.
Heart pounding, I spoke the words.
You said "yes" and the magic began.

I barely said a word to you next day
in class, though my blush betrayed
me and told all as Ms. Taylor read
a passage from "Romeo and Juliet ".

I turn the faded pages of my yearbook
into a fairy tale. You in white jacket
with boutonniere, me in white organza,
with delicate pink embroidery.

My hands caress a pressed corsage,
fragile, and faded. Your presence escapes
to a place in my being where the scent
of gardenias linger. One perfect night.

Magic

Look at her. She's laughing at his jokes.
Not very original. What is she hearing?
Look at him transfixed by her smile.
Ordinary. What does he see?

I take their order. He asks for a beer,
she a glass of Chardonnay. He strokes
her flowing blond hair. She sees
no one but him amid the noisy crowd.

I return with their drinks. "You don't
have to watch chic flicks for me," she says.
He is impressed, so taken with her
selflessness. He responds, "no problem."

Tender blossoms of budding love
vowed to last forever, sparked with giddiness,
caught up in bliss. A sudden fall
into love some call magic, others trickery.

Winter's Frost

An orange grove claimed by winter
frost. A chill wraps its icy grasp
around juicy fruit the promise
of sweet, refreshing nectar. Gold

and rust chrysanthemums bloom, under
sunlight, then wither and die leaving
behind crumpled, brown weeds. She lets
them lie there. How quickly admiration

turns to tolerance…finally apathy. Secretly
she yearns for that "butterflies in the stomach"
feeling again. Fantasies of the handsome
UPS guy bring a fleeting moment

of contentment. She sets a glass of orange
juice before her lover. He reads the
newspaper with a keen eye for women's
intimate clothing ads. He says,
"This orange juice has lost its taste."

Wedding Cup

We toast the groom and bride.
May peace and love in you
abide. As you drink
from this cup of
holy libation
your
vows will join
you
in
a
life
of
joy
and
celebration.

Sacred Sense

(Dedicated to Helen Keller and Anne Sullivan)

She cradles a doll tenderly with sacred
sense of touch giving spirit to the silent
darkness of her world. The bond
between student and teacher a magical
door opened to life and love. Dear
companions they share a miracle
sparked by hope and patience.

Is there a message for me? Touch
me with your soul. Show me how
to see without eyes, to hear without
ears, to speak words that break
barriers of ego, apathy and prejudice.
Share with me your enlightenment.
Thus the student becomes the teacher.

Broken Wings

Do small things with great love

I walk the slums of Calcutta.

I see them all around like parakeets

with broken wings that need mending.

So many of them needing food, clean

water and care. Listless eyes filled

with pain. Hopeless faces begging

compassion and bread.

It is not I who deserve humanitarian

awards but the poor, the sick

and abandoned who are suffering.

Never enough money, time or medicine

to heal their wounds. Is there no divine

intervention of a loving God? Some

times I doubt. My faith is tested.

I feel as abandoned as those I try

to help. Even so I am driven to go on.

Storyteller

My friend has a gift. She plays her words
like finely-tuned keys on a baby grand.
Onomatopoeic sounds punctuate her tales
with "quack-quacks", "vrooooms" and whinnies.

Whispered words slowly rise to crescendo!
"What, when, where?" Revelation bursts
forth with a perfectly timed "boo" or "crash".
Bright-eyed children share the moment.

The teller of tales embodies wonder and joy.
Her symphony sanctifies marriage
of melody and word, fantasy and fact.
My friend is a minstrel, a bard, a blessing.

Jane's Kitchen

Magic morsels of berried
confection, miniature loaves
of contentment. Bounty of rich
harvest and compassion merged,
bestowing spiritual sustenance
upon those who partake.

Sugared bits of life offered
as bread for the soul. Treasure
created in the floured sanctuary,
unpretentious in its great gift,
a reflection of her unassuming manner.
These are the gifts consecrated
in the kindness of Jane's kitchen.

Phyllis

Quietly she goes about her day
as the sun rising and setting, without
pomp or ceremony as if it were nothing
magnificent—sacred. In faithful covenant
she walks her journey caring for those
in need of His love. All done with light-hearted
humor as though nothing remarkable were
taking place. Such is her "fiat", such is her
offering, such is her communion with His will—
the greatness of her glorious triumph.

Furlough
(For Paul)

I rinsed soap off the last dinner plate, placed it in
the rack.

You checked your duffle bag.

A part of me was feeling empty, another felt a
sense of relief knowing life would be less chaotic.

You played a video game called Utopia.

I watched you build a perfect world.

Your ride to the airport arrived.

"Take care of yourself."

I watched you leave.

Antilogy

The primal pulse of my existence stirs.
She is the universe. She is God. She lives.

My childhood cries aloud in need,
trusting in her omnipresence. She lives.

In adolescent turmoil I tolerate
her presence, and, yet, she lives.

Then, in paradox and parallel, her echo
I become. So well, she lives.

Seasoned now, both she and I, no
filial masks we wear. She dies.

Love

Some describe love as butterflies in the stomach.
Sounds suspiciously like indigestion to me.

Others say it's being ga-ga over someone.
Now what could that mean? Baby talk?

There are those who tell of being head
over heels, a rather peculiar position.

What about people who are in La-la land?
Must be just outside Emerald City.

Some simply fall in love which may
Result in broken body parts. Is having

a crush anything like eating a Sundae?
Could it be that true love has little to do with
feelings?

Nature

Resurrection

Snow

Delicate flakes

Falling from above

Creation's bit of magic

Mirth

Rain

Powerful, transparent

Drenching, cleansing, purging

Natural author of events

Master

Waiting

Lilies budding

Earth offering promise

Surrendering to creation

New life!

One, Tiny Snowflake

Rooftops lightly dusted with white
flakes of snow like cupcakes sprinkled
with powdered sugar. Intricate patterns,
one of a kind fashioned by a master craftsman.
Willing, as thousands of others, to surrender
unique shape to a carrot-nosed snowman.

The hidden promise of spring protected
by a silent white blanket. Like joy it flies
by and beckons to be caught by the spirit
of wonder and imagination. Lasting
for an instant, living in the moment, content
with its existence. One, tiny snowflake.

Promise

I saw it! I did!
There it was amid
mighty lightning
and thunderous rumble.
It was green and red,
yellow and purple.
A great arc, beauty painted
on dismal, ebony sky.

Ba-boom—thunder roared,
lightning threatened,
hailstones fell. A burst
of mystical beauty, undaunted
in the awesome power
of nature's might, existing
side by side. Radiant
rainbow in the darkness.
Promise of hope.

Essence

Essence of the rose.

Beauty which words fail to speak.

Behold nature's gift.

Kite

Wind's search for mischief
scatters leaves here and about,
seeking a playmate.

See the kite ascend,
a colorful, tiny speck
caught in the current.

The boy far below
cleverly navigating
elated and free.

Bless the Beasts

Do they know what they bring us,

the comfort and laughter?

Can they sense in our mood

a before and an after?

Their coming and going,

so simple a treasure

to us such a gift

that is far beyond measure.

When they offer a paw

can they know what it means

to a hand still abundant

with hopes and with dreams?

Can their eyes meet with ours

and not feel each our story

of joy and of sadness

of wisdom and glory?

Falling Back

There is sadness in the air.
Reminiscent aromas. Firecrackers,
hot dogs and barbecued ribs.
Summer picnics. The hours

fall back and old Sol glows in another
place and time. Like a wandering
gypsy he sets at different
campsites, seasonal obedience

ceasing his glow early in the day.
Time for candlelight, deep thought,
poetry, and keeping warm. Flowers
disappear like hibernating bears.

Soon there will be a festival
of lights, symbol of hope, followed
by the winter prelude to spring.
But today there is sadness in the air.

Seedlings

He stood before the vineyard, vast

and lovely, with blossoms of a bounty

yet to bloom. The grapes were plentiful.

The sweet, comforting fragrance

reminded him of his people so far away.

He thought how pleased they would be

he had planted their treasured seed

in this new land with its fertile soil,

wide valleys and abundant sun.

Today is a good day!

Prelude

The sun slowly sets
painting the evening sky's hue.
Prelude to darkness.

White

White is a gracious hostess
allowing her guests to dazzle in splendor.
A backdrop for an azure sky, floral bouquet,
or marching band bedecked in brightly
colored finery. Would her sisters
glow without her hospitality?

I admire white,
the cornerstone of all colors.
She beckons her siblings
to take up residency. A vacant
canvas, she sings solitary beauty
in her own unassuming way.

White. Tabula rasa for artist's brush
and author's pen. Unadorned.
Generous. Simple. White
accommodates life's diversity.
She is my heroine!

Journey

Change

Change: It's a multifaceted word.

It's capricious and fickle and sometimes

absurd.

We have changes of clothing and changes of

heart.

Emotional changes causes lovers to part.

An attitude change is most welcome at

times.

We make change for a dollar with nickels

and dimes.

The change in the weather doth allergies

make.

As the changeable earth with tremors does

quake.

The Brits change babies' royal nappies with

care,

While movie stars alter their color of hair.

We change places of residence, cars and
professions,
Hairdressers, lawyers, and even obsessions.
When we think we've adjusted to all
situations,
More changes occur much to our
trepidation.

Life's Music

Beep...beep...beep. The steady beat
of a monitor welcomed me to
life with the rhythmic pulse of my heart.
My piercing cry said, "Let me be part
of the symphony." Da-da-da-da...
Ba-ba-ba...forming words from
sounds like rhymes in a Dr. Seuss
book. Intonation as notes on sheet
music resulted in masterpieces.

Nursery rhymes, magical tonic
for the soul, nourished my childhood.
Then came adolescence and a rock 'n' roll
explosion sensual and freeing. Waking
a dormant consciousness folk songs
of the sixties changed a generation
of baby boomers into caring activists.
On to disco, R&B and Hip Hop.

Content now with hymns
and what my children call
"elevator music" my rocking
chair keeps an age appropriate
swing to life's pace. I visualize
myself playing heaven's iconic
harp at my final destination.
I hope to leave on a good note.

Dollhouse

It wasn't made of wood like old
fashioned ones. Not oak nor cherry
nor maple. But rather of metal as a Sears
Roebuck pre-fab construction.
The kitchen's formica-topped table
offered miniature portions of orange juice
and oatmeal prepared by an aproned-
mother for her carefully molded
children. Father looked on in approval.
In the bedroom lay a tiny rug, giving
warmth to little feet on a frosty morning.
The family of my childhood dream.

The house and furniture have long
ago been discarded. After all
grown-ups don't play with toys.
There are bills to be paid, noses
to wipe, children to feed, floors
to be scrubbed and laundry to do.
No—grown-ups don't play with toys.

Annie's Reunion

Annie, an orphan framed by her youth,
would never grow old, nor her red hair turn silver.
Applauded by thousands yet confined by boundary,
She stepped out of the box toward a page called life.

She met people with nametags; uncles and cousins created
by power more sacred than those of ink-pen or brush.
A family reunion; a gathering of clan rich in bonding.
Midst aromas of chowder and sweet corn she mingled.

"Are you my father? Is your name mom?"
Empty stares answered wide-eyes.
In comical banter pain is hidden.
"Life isn't fair, but I don't care!"

Back to the box, clothed in solitary, red
dress, protective armor against reality's sting.
The box, where revision pens joy from sorrow.
No mother, no dad. Reunions are sad.

Sister Souls

We share a laugh, my sisters and I,
Some tears we shed 'tis true.
Our sharing makes the burden light
And hope and dreams renew.

How blessed is this bond we share
Of fear, of joy and weeping.
Our sister souls rejoice as one
Each other's vigil keeping.

With courage borne of one another
We meet the coming tide
Besieged by life's capricious woes
Its roaring crest we ride.

Our lighted candles burn sustained.
We pledge in silent vow,
To spark the flame that flickers
Thus our covenant bestow.

And just as winds of time erode
Earth's beauty old to new
So does the mighty gust of storm
Unfold our splendor too.

Magnificent as trees of oak
With barren, broken limbs
Anointing each the other's wounds
With praising, sister hymns.

Grandma's Wedding Dress

Adorned in white lace you stand,
so much wisdom to share. I gaze
at your image, envision you walking
through time to unravel a mystery,
your story. I know so little about

you. What emotions lie hidden
beneath solemn face and formal
pose: love, pride, joy, anxiety?
Feelings veiled in propriety
glimmer through like wisps

of hair peeking out at your cheek.
I see courage and compassion,
sadness and joy, wisdom
and acceptance. You begin
a new life—a life that will course
through my veins in years to come.

Aunt Tillie

Crazy Aunt Tillie is what we called her behind
her back. She was generous to a fault, roaming
through the dollar stores, buying plastic toys,
trinkets for nieces and nephews, doling them
out like gold and silver treasures. On special
days love was pizza with meatballs and cheese.

When chicken was on sale she bought three
or four to make huge pots of chicken soup
never served. After three weeks it was offered
to Tippy, her dog, who walked away from
the bowl of questionable liquid.

Tillie once proudly walked into the voting booth
and realized she voted for FDR's opponent
in error so she made a scene. When she removed
the Christmas tree in March the dried branches
shed thousands of pine needles likening the room
to a campsite.

I cherish the antique gold looking glass she gave me. A round mirror on each side framed in an intricate gold stand. I see my reflection changing over the years. Wisps of gray hair and crow's feet: genetic markers. I wonder what the future holds for me. I try not to think about the day Tillie was taken away in restraints.

Anticipation

I sit and ponder.

Life breathes itself to being

From where is the source?

I wait for patience.

It answers not my beckon.

I helplessly wait.

Flawless

The rug maker diligently weaves
a defect into his work confirming
perfection belongs only to the divine.

A cracked clay pot trickles
water down upon dry wild flowers
on its journey from the river.

So beautiful the butterfly
as it struggles its way
out of drab, dull cocoon.

All with blemish are not flawed.
Destined for greater glory
within the Creator's hands.

Laura

In wide-eyed beauty she begins
her pilgrimage as infant, toddler,
adolescent. Step by step, joyously
dancing paths of bride, lover, friend, mother.
With blush on her cheeks paled by life's
capricious whims, she remains
a vibrant star in the Creator's galaxy.
Having given her precious cup of compassion
to those graced by her presence she offers
her "fiat" in serene acceptance, aware
that we have been changed by her existence.
Fragile as the gently blooming orchid yet
sturdy as a great oak she goes forward
again wide-eyed to begin her journey.

Hands

Hands that nurtured babies,
strummed music with delight,
kneaded bread, mended clothes.

Hands no longer smooth,
arthritic and twisted, worn
by everyday toil and time.

Hands folded in prayer
Praising God—reaching out
to a sister or brother

for help. More beautiful
than ever, sanctified
by imperfection.

Carnival

"Why do you worry?" asks
the bearded lady. "We are what we are."
Admission bought with confusion,
I enter the tent of enigma
into a dreamlike carnival.

The barker is hawking humanity's litany.
The fat lady gobbles
up my anxiety, the fire-eater
my passion. Layers of hidden thoughts
are torn as the geek eats away at my brain.

Regrets invade my mind like sticky
cotton candy which must be washed away.
The intricate designs on the tattooed man
so simple, yet perplexing, poignant
messages begging for interpretation.

I watch the sword of acceptance
being swallowed. Only then does
a distant calliope's lullaby return
me to serenity, dreamless sleep.
Respite from my introspective pilgrimage.

Made in the USA
Charleston, SC
28 September 2014